Mary J. Pryor

Start Now!

Life Is Too Short

the Pryor Group
Yukon, Oklahoma

Copyright © 1995 by Mary J. Pryor

Published by the Pryor Group
           Yukon, Oklahoma

No part of this book may be reproduced by any mechanical, photographic, or electronic process, or in the form of a phonographic recording, nor may it be stored in a retrieval system, transmitted, or otherwise copied for public or private use without the written permission of the publisher.

First printing: June 1995
Second printing: March 1997

Library of Congress Catalogue Card Number 95-92312

ISBN 1-887587-01-2

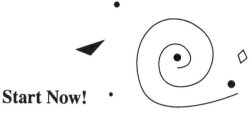

Start Now!
Life Is Too Short

Art by Donna Carpenter

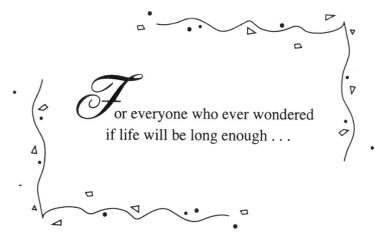

For everyone who ever wondered if life will be long enough . . .

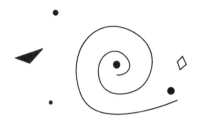

The ideas I stand for are not mine.
I borrowed them from Socrates.
I swiped them from Chesterfield.
I stole them from Jesus.
And I put them in a book.
If you don't like their rules,
whose would you use?
—Dale Carnegie

One day I'll be old. And that's O.K.
One day you'll be old too.
That's probably part of the plan.

But I want to be old and happy.
Old and content.
Old, with no regrets.

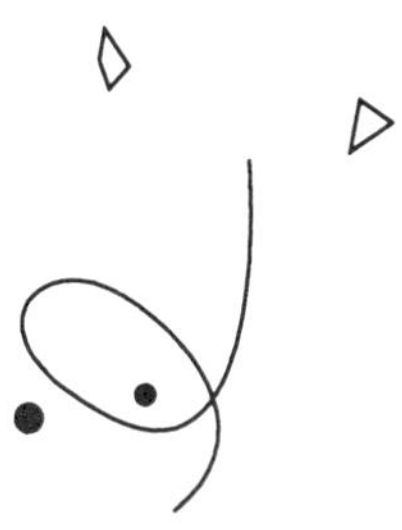

*Whatever became
of the person
I was hoping to become?*

–Ashleigh Brilliant

I do not want regrets,
broken dreams,
shattered visions,
great unused ideas,
promises I made to myself and never kept,
excuses about why I never did
 all the things I should have done.

I do not want to hear myself saying
"Life was just too short!"

And I certainly don't want to be embarrassed
about all I had, or owned, or possessed,
and didn't use.

Life is too short for that.

$\mathcal{I}$t's too short to be saying things like:

I wish I'd remembered . . .

I wish I'd thought to . . .

I wish I'd given . . .

I wish I'd known . . .

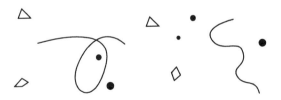

Life is too short to worry.

Do you like me?
Have I made you mad?
Will people accept my ideas?
Are my clothes good enough?
Am I socially correct?
Did that absentminded clerk
    count my change correctly?
Did the pizza arrive in fifteen minutes or less,
    as guaranteed?

Life is too short to worry.
Stop timing the pizza man!!

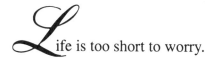

*L*ife is too short.

Let go of anger.

Let go of hate.

Let go of fear.

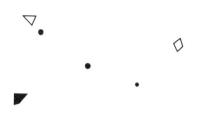

Hang on to joy!

Hang on to life!

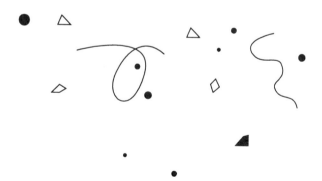

If life is too short to worry,
life is also too short *not* to trust.

It's too short not to accept your apology,
because maybe you weren't sincere enough.

It's too short not to believe promises, just because
I've been let down before.

It's too short to wonder what you really meant
when you said what you said.

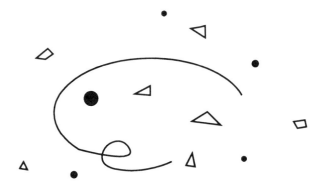

*L*ife is too short to offer advice
from the passenger seat of your car,
when the adult to your left
has physical control of the car
and you are supposed to be along for the ride.

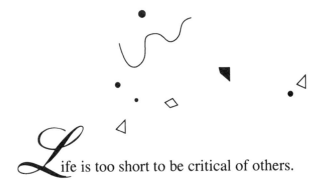

*L*ife is too short to be critical of others.

Life is for concentrating on you,
      and letting life unfold for other people
          as it will.

If life is too short not to trust people,
it's also too short not to act.

Life is too short not to give gifts of yourself,
often and freely.

*Give what you have,
It might be better
than you dare to think.*

      –H.W. Longfellow

𝓛ife is too short not to buy flowers
for the people you love,

and that includes you!

*L*ife is too short to say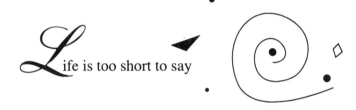

"Yeah, well, I wish I could help you."

*L*ife is too short not to spoil your pet.

Even if the dog ate your lunch bag,
>and the peanut butter sandwich still inside.

Extra attention and hugs qualify
for spoiled treatment.
So does just a little more time, just for them.

Animals ask so little.
They give so much.

Life is too short *not* to drink in sunset

                    after sunset

                        after sunset.

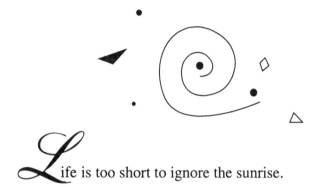

*L*ife is too short to ignore the sunrise.

Catch it tomorrow.
It is playing in your neighborhood.

*Time flies like an arrow.
Fruit flies like a banana.*

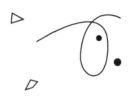

ife is too short

not to take your loved ones by total surprise.

Life is too short to put off writing letters
to grandbabies still unborn.

Life is too short to rush the seasons.

Life is too short to decorate for Christmas

on Thanksgiving Day,

and undecorate the morning of December 26.

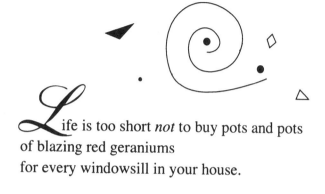

*L*ife is too short *not* to buy pots and pots of blazing red geraniums for every windowsill in your house.

In January.

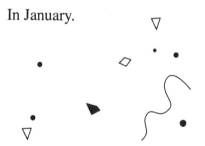

$\mathcal{L}$ife is too short for your pictures and
memories to be permanently hidden
in shoeboxes and dresser drawers.

Buy an outrageous number of picture frames
and flaunt your relatives and friends.

Thirty or so small framed pictures
would be a nice start.

ife is too short

    –to forget to tell people you love them.

    Often.

    –to forget to show them you love them.

    Often.

*Gratitude without words
is gratitude
never heard.*

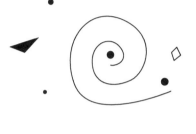

*L*ife is too short *not* to give away
twice as much money
as you think you can afford,
anonymously.

*L*ife is too short *not* to say thank you
    to people who have shaped your life.

Life is too short not to acknowledge those
    who have helped you on your way.

Stop.

Do one *thank you* now.

No excuses.

Telephone or stationery required.
You have both.

✳✳✳ **Proper etiquette for thank yous** ✳✳✳

- required for things that make you smile

- imperative for letting people know you noticed

- highly acceptable at any time

*E*ven if there's not a reason to say thank you . . .

Life is too short not to be kind.
Even to the surly, churlish, crabby, and mean.

*L*ife is too short to let go of childhood.

To act crazy,
dramatic,
to imagine you're someone you're not
       –just for a while.

To stop giving spontaneous hugs.

To work instead of play,

To stop licking the ice cream off the dasher.

To use a boring rubber spatula
instead of your finger
to lick the frosting bowl clean.

$\mathcal{I}$f life is too short to let go of childhood
Hold on!

I hope you are holding on.

I hope you're still
    -unafraid of being different
    -certain of love and friendship
    -surrounded by the things
        that make you happy.

What were those things
that made you happy as a child?

Where are the toys that were warmth, and safety,
and caring, and joy to you then?

Where's your teddy now? Your dolly? Your train set?

Get them out of the attic, out of storage,
out of their boxes.
They are still a part of you.

Who said history has to be packed away?

Life is for celebrating good memories
and good feelings.

*People do not quit playing
because they grow old.
They grow old
because they quit playing.*
                                        —*Oliver Wendell Holmes*
(who played until his death at age ninety-three)

𝓛ife is too short
to pack away the good things in boxes.

You are never too old for toys.

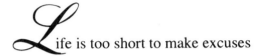
Life is too short to make excuses

          I forgot.

          You never told me.

          I planned on it.

          I ran out of time.

          He never asked.

          I never asked.

*L*ife is too short-
but that doesn't mean I have to do everything.

It's not my life work to reform people
who are suffering from terminal grumpiness.

I don't have to buy in to gloom and doom.

I don't have to feel guilty.

Life is too short to work at work.

Breathe.

Take time off.

Smile.

Keep your perspective.

Tell your boss you're following the advice of C.W. Metcalf–

*Lighten Up and Live
or Tighten Up and Leave*

*L*ife is too short *not* to take risks.

Now is the best time
of your life
for a wild leap into
your future.

Do something today
you never thought
you'd have the courage
to do.

Start now!

"There is no use trying," said Alice.
"One can't believe impossible things."

"I dare say you haven't much
practice," said the Queen.
"When I was your age,
I always did it
for half an hour a day.
Why, sometimes, I've believed
as many as six impossible things before
breakfast."

-Lewis Carroll

Alice In Wonderland

$\mathcal{U}$p until now, this book has only required that you use three things: your eyes, your brain, and your heart. From this point on, it will require two more things: a pen or pencil *that you will use,* and your personal commitment to actually answer any questions that follow.

O.K.?
Committed?
Ready . . .
Set . . .
Go!

*Q*uick.
Make a list right here of everything you'd like to do in your life. Really.
Do It Now!

———————————

———————————

———————————

———————————

———————————

———————————

Please pause here.

Look at your list on the last page,
and answer yourself honestly–

How many of those things have you done?

Any of them?

Half of them?

All of them?

Have you started them only in your head?

*If you don't get started,
you won't get finished.*

Like me and a lot of other people,
you probably procrastinate about some things.

The trouble comes when we procrastinate about things that could change our lives.

*Life
is what happens to you
when you're busy
making other plans.*

　　　　　　　　　　–John Lennon

The experts say we procrastinate for a lot of reasons.

Check any of the following that are true for you.

- ○ inability to analyze or prioritize
- ○ fatigue
- ○ depression
- ○ forgetfulness
- ○ anxiety
- ○ dependence on others

But it's simpler than that.
We procrastinate because we're human.

And humans are often afraid. Afraid to fail.

What if people laugh at me?

What if they think I'm stupid?

What if I can't do it?

What if nobody likes me

What if I lose all my money?

But we humans are also sometimes afraid
—to succeed.

What if people expect this every time?

What if I can't do this again?

What if my friends won't like me anymore?

What if they won't like me for myself?

Maybe you'd like to write down the reasons
you've put some things off for such a long time:
- ○
- ○
- ○
- ○
- ○

Colors

*Your living is determined
not so much
by what life brings to you
as by the attitude you bring to life:
not so much
by what happens to you
as by the way
your mind looks at what happens.
Circumstances and situations
do color your life,
but you have been given the mind
to choose what the color shall be.*

—John Homer Miller

𝓑ut forgetting about procrastination and not having done as much as we one day want to do, the real question for you and me is . . .

**What are you going to do about it?
What in the world
are you going to do about it?**

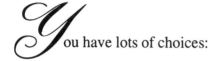ou have lots of choices:

You could forget it.

You could excuse it.

You could laugh about it.

You could lose this book.
 (the author discourages this option)
You could blame it on someone or something else.

You could blame yourself.

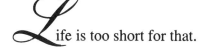 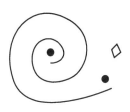

*L*ife is too short for that.

It's too short for anything except action.

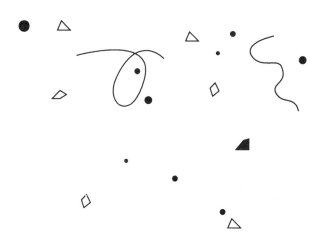

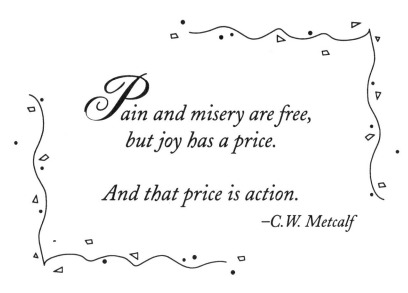

*Pain and misery are free,
but joy has a price.*

And that price is action.
—C.W. Metcalf

What are you waiting for?

>your mother's permission?

>your children's approval?

>your colleagues' full support and understanding?

>a truckload of courage?

>sharper pencils?

>better clothes?

>newer paints?

>a more opportune time?

>more time to practice?

>a little time to prepare?

>a lot of time to prepare?

>some time to think about it?

You don't need any of those things.

All you need to do is take action!

Start now!

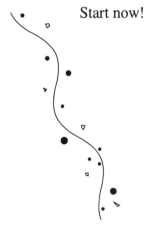

Life is too short to wait much longer.

No, life is too short to wait any longer.
Now is the time to act on your dreams.

According to a study from Cornell University, it is the things they have failed to do, that people regret the most. Failing to act was the biggest regret of their lives.

In another Cornell study, researchers found that actions that turn out badly may cause more pain in the short run, but inaction may be regretted more in the long run.

Why? We may be afraid to try.

As we get older, we grow more confident. Maybe assuming we could have done just fine, we end up feeling worse for not having done something.

ime
for more pencil lead and personal commitment.

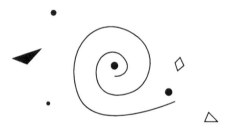

Here's a place for your plan:

> I've decided life *is* too short.
> So I'm starting now.

Here's my plan:

In the next week, (   ) I'll:

O

O

O

and next month, (   ) I'm going to:

O

O

O

O

O

in six months, (   ) I will have:

O

O

O

O

O

and one year from now,   (   ) I:

○

○

○

○

○

You did notice the spaces for you to write in the dates? That's part of your contract with yourself.

When you reach a goal, write the actual date beside that goal. Check it off.
Better yet, paste a star, color a picture, sprinkle glitter all around it.

You deserve it! You've done something about life being too short.

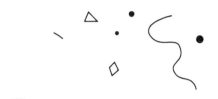

Goals don't work unless you do.

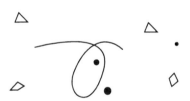

You need this record you can see of *everything*

✓ you've planned to do,

✓ thought about doing,

✓ promised yourself you'd do,

✓ and actually did.

*The palest ink
is better than the best memory.*

Someone said, "Words crystallize thoughts."

Words move your thoughts and wishes into reality.

And speaking of reality,
        life is too short to wait much longer.

*Somebody should tell us
we are dying.
Then we might live life to the limit,
every minute of every day.
Do it!
Whatever you want to do,
do it now.
There are only so many tomorrows.*

–Michael Landon

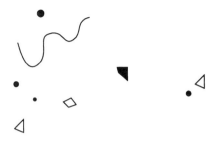

$\mathcal{M}$aybe I should wait until I'm better,
a little more perfect?

Not a good idea.

You don't have to be perfect to start anything,
and you don't have to put things off
until you're sure you can perform them flawlessly.

Life is too short for that.

Using Norman Vincent Peale's advice, Ray Dupont pictures his life as a construction site, with a sign at the site reading

UNDER CONSTRUCTION

Just like those endless stretches of road in the summer, those detours the Highway Department builds into your summer vacation. (What did you think they did in the winter? That's when they plan how to disrupt summer travel on every highway in the nation. It is a very serious job.)

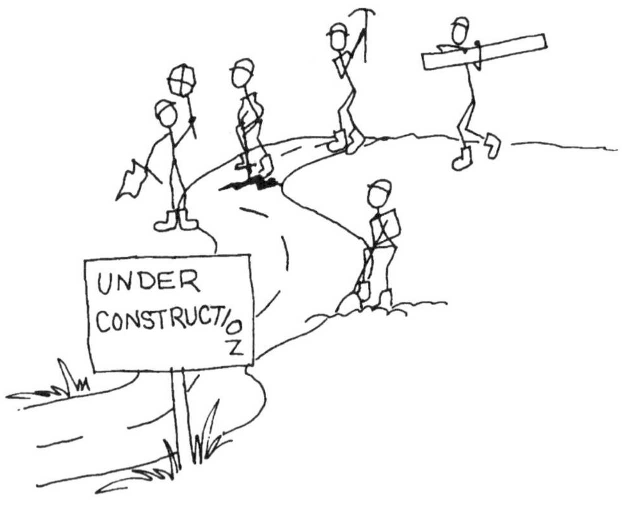
UNDER
CONSTRUCTION

But Ray says the sign for his life will change once he nears life's end. He wants his epitaph to read:

> **Construction complete.**
> **Thank you for your patience.**

That's all we need to ask of people-a little patience as we grow, and take chances,
and live out our dreams.

$\mathcal{R}$ay doesn't want his epitaph to read:

**Construction complete.
Thank you for judging me harshly,
holding me
to my own high standards of perfectionism.
Thank you for keeping me from taking chances
and fulfilling my dreams.**

No one expects perfection from you, except you.

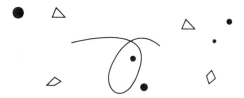

So maybe it's time,
to start now

before life really is too short.

Health Benefit

You'll get a burst of energy
when you decide to get started.

Health Caution

Life is definitely too short for you to say:

>But I don't have the time.

>I don't have the money.

>I've got too much to do at this time of my life.

>I don't have enough. . .
>(add your favorite excuse here)

o...
how much longer
are you going to wait before you start?

When you find yourself saying, "I can't, because", ask yourself: So?

        So what?

        What am I going to do about it?

*Insanity
is expecting things to improve
while you continue
to do the same thing.*

$\mathcal{L}$ook closely at your wish list, way back on page 46. Study the things you want, even if those wishes are still only inside of your head.

(It would be easier to write these thoughts down—you wouldn't have to roll your eyes up in your head to look at them!)

Are you willing to start making payments?

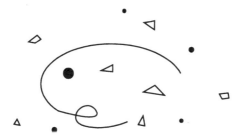

Portia Davis thinks that people have high and false expectations for their dreams. Most people, she says, mentally tack up their wish lists to the front of their refrigerators, and then they wait.

All year, every year, they wait. They wait for someone to look at the list, choose an item, and make that particular dream come true.

They somehow think that as a birthday or anniversary present, someone will give them what they want.

Portia says the list never gets shorter that way. It just stays the same.

> The only way to get things from the list is to
> **START MAKING THE PAYMENTS.**

And no one except you can make those payments.

*L*ook at the things you've put on hold. Pick one thing, just one, and start making the payments on it NOW!

Start now!

Don't select a major life change, just choose an action–different or more than you would have done, before you read this book.

start small.

What about that phone call to a friend?

A card to your mother?

Extra hugs and cuddles for your kids tonight?

Flowers for yourself?

*W*ait!
Somebody is saying, "Well, of course, I'm going to get started and do those things, but right now I've got to walk the dog, buy groceries, make my meeting, and get some sleep."

Sound like someone you know?

If you've no time to do it now, you might as well be dead. What difference will it make?

You're not doing the things you want to do.

Choosing not to do it or not being able to do it– either way, it's not getting done.

Are you too busy?
If you put your wishes and dreams aside, even for a minute, I guarantee that they will quietly remain there, to the side, not making one tiny peep.

Additionally, I guarantee that they will still be there when you take them out to look at them from time to time.

And they won't complain.

They won't warn you or threaten you or deliver a ***now or never*** ultimatum. They'll just continue to patiently wait until you are ready to act.

*The dictionary
is the only place
success
comes before
work.*

*In life,
it's the other way around.*

Feeling guilty? Read on.

You're the only one standing in your way.

Just you.
Not me, not your family, not time.
We may take your attention away
from the problem, but you're the one
with the solution.

Keep telling me about your busy stressful life.
You elaborate on it, I'll commiserate with you,
and soon both of us will have forgotten
the big question, which is:

Why aren't you doing something now?

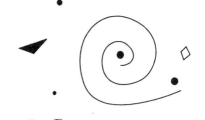

The future comes one day at a time. And today comes one hour at a time.

But those hours get lost easily.

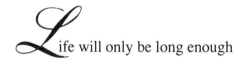ife will only be long enough

when you and I have

whittled down our lists,

made our connections,

earned our peace,

delivered on our promises.

Growing up, we'd get fresh eggs from my aunt Mildred. She and her family lived four miles from us, not a great distance when you're raised in the country.

Mildred is my Mom's sister. Mom would pile all five of us kids into the car and we'd tool over to Mildred's house. And Mildred's work, whatever she was doing when she saw us drive up, would stop. She'd smile, and we'd all sit down in the kitchen or lean against the fence outside and she and Mom would talk. Being kids, we'd soon run off to play with our cousins. It all seemed normal at the time. But from this perspective, it seems unusual and rare. Drop what you're doing, with grace, with a smile, and enjoy just what that moment brought you? I'm sure at times, visitors were welcome breaks, but there had to be many more times that Mildred must have wished the work hadn't been interrupted. Huge gardens to tend, and harvest, and put up every day in the summer; laundry for a family of eight, done in a washhouse thirty feet from the house; six kids and a farmer husband to prepare meals for, usually at odd hours. She never ran out of work.

*S*o, here I sit in my busy life, peeved sometimes by interruptions, not wanting to take time now for something or someone, promising "later, we'll do that later."

I need to remember Mildred. She was busier than I've ever been, physically exhausted from a daily schedule I couldn't maintain for more than a week, with a workday that was
consistent only in two things–the physical toll it took and the long hours it required.

Of course, she and Mom were sisters, glad to see each other, and they saw each other
frequently. Still, Mildred always stopped, always smiled.

That picture is still clear to me.

It was evidently clear to her too,
that life is too short.

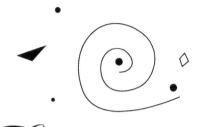

*The best things in life
are better
than the other things.*

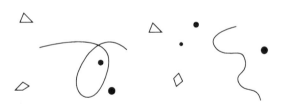

Are the gremlins in your head making noise now? Can you hear them?

What if?

What would happen?

How would I?

I don't have the talent.

I don't have enough money.

We'd never pull it off.

I don't know how.

Life is too short to make excuses.

If I had my life to live over

*I would have invited friends
over to dinner
even if the carpet was stained
and the sofa faded.*

*I would have eaten popcorn
in the "good" living room
and worried
much less about the dirt
when someone wanted
to light a fire in the fireplace.*

*I would have sat on the lawn with
my children
and not worried about grass stains.*
　　　　　　　　　　　　　–Erma Bombeck

*J*ust tell that to the gremlins in your head,
   then thank them,
and shut the door gently
as you push them into a mental closet.

Preferably one
with a lock on the
outside.

Life is too short
   not to take the risks.

But I'm too old to change.

There's too much in place in my life!

—Some of Us

"Of course, I can make changes,
I just can't make major life changes now!"

Those gremlins have you worried about that?

You can change!

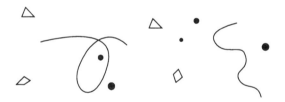

*D*r. Herbert Lenaburg was 26 years old and not a doctor at all.

He'd been a farmer all of his life, and a successful one. His farm was paid for, and he felt dissatisfied.

"I felt I should be doing more with what I had. So, I surrendered myself to do whatever the Lord wanted me to do. I had been successful at preaching, so my minister felt that I was called to preach. I told him that I felt I was called to do something, I just wasn't sure what it was. "

Herbert Lenaburg decided to go to college and get an education. He enrolled in Oklahoma Baptist University.

"I put my farm up for sale and sold out of farming. At that time my children were small, one four years old, one 6 months of age."

"My minister had introduced me as a ministerial student, so I got the opportunity to preach."

Only Herbert felt that the sermons weren't working. He felt that nothing was coming together, that nothing was working out, even with a straight A scholastic average.

He was in turmoil. He had sold his farm, changed his life, and now everything seemed wrong. His answer came to him during a softball game.

He was playing softball with the church team, and trying to catch a line drive, six inches off the ground. The ball hit and dislocated two fingers. His minister came over, looked at the fingers, and said "That's not going to hurt you-it won't hurt to have those fingers crooked. It's happened to me."

"That was the first time I said, 'I can't have crooked fingers.' My hand was never x-rayed. Although I'd been told my fingers would be sore for at least a week, they were never sore at all."

He left the game with an injured hand, and a lot of determination.

"I went into medicine. even though my advisor said there was no way I could make it through medical school with a family. But everything straightened out and went well. No questions, no problems."

Looking for a place to practice, he chose the Baptist Hospital in Mangum, Oklahoma. A missionary there at the time told him, "We have been praying for months for a Baptist minister to come to Mangum."

Dr. Lenaburg is now retired, more than thirty years after he started following his heart.

On the great clock of time,
there's but one word,

and that word
is
now!

Start now!

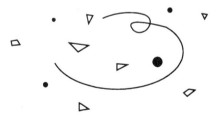

I hope I have left you

with a clutch of second thoughts,

a flight of yesterdays,

a twinkling of todays,

and a promise of tomorrows.

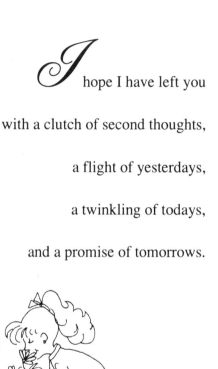

Mary J. Pryor is a member of the Pryor Group, a company dedicated to building people personally and professionally through training in motivation, communication, planning, and goal setting.

What have you done about life being too short? Mary would love to hear from you.

>Mary J. Pryor
>the Pryor Group
>
>(405) 354-1604
>pryorgp@icnet.net